Knocking on the Earth

WESLEYAN NEW POETS

Knocking on the Earth

Ellery Akers

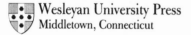
Wesleyan University Press
Middletown, Connecticut

Some of these poems appeared originally in *The Aspen Anthology, The California Quarterly, Harvard Magazine, Ploughshares,* and *Three Rivers Poetry Journal.* Three poems have won awards from the Poetry Society of America: "Letters to Anna: 1846–54," 1980 John Masefield Award; "Advice from an Angel," 1984 John Masefield Award; "Night: Volcano, California," 1985 Gordon Barber Award.

Thanks are due to the MacDowell Colony for several fellowships that made it possible for me to complete this book.

All inquiries and permissions requests should be addressed to the Publisher, Wesleyan University Press, 110 Mt. Vernon Street, Middletown, Connecticut 06457.

Library of Congress Cataloging-in-Publication Data

Akers, Ellery, 1946–
    Knocking on the earth.
    (Wesleyan new poets)
    I. Title. II. Series.
PS3551.K44K6 1989   811'.54   88-26081
ISBN 0-8195-2161-2
ISBN 0-8195-1162-5 (pbk.)

Manufactured in the United States of America

FIRST EDITION
Wesleyan New Poets

for Cecily Corcoran Kihn, Peter Kunz, and Marjorie Harris

. . . I knock on the earth for my friend.
—HENRY DAVID THOREAU

Contents

I

Time Passing, Many Afternoons

Night: Volcano, California

I have been walking for hours on a street called Consolation,
near Jerome, Emigrant, National,
past lit houses with orchards and hoses, where meals are being laid,
and in the yellow squares the figures waver,
while out here, I realize, once again, I am alone.
Tonight I don't mind so much. A porch light cuts into the darkness
    like steam,
and falls oddly on an aluminum shed, a red roof suddenly pale,
a toolbox, a child's bicycle.
I think of my friends, lifting me across the years,
while the Plough and the Archer follow each other
at exactly the same distance every night,
and the Swan floats and points its long neck,
and the Oaks drowse, Valleys and Blues.

All day I have been reading
about the invisible world, the one
that's always trying to reach us. What if we could hear
the small round *o*'s of dirt,
the chant of stars and plants,
carbon and sulphur, calling to each other, innumerable
to innumerable, a throat at every blade of grass.

A dog walks up Emigrant,
smelling his way home, sniffs me, barks,
And it seems to me now that the night is a sea, is a mouth,
full of fish, full of trees, viburnum smelling like turpentine,
catalpas thrashing into the wind with their cargo of pods and stars,

and I don't miss the day, though the pole I'm holding in my hand
has turned cold and black as a fossil, and the road seems packed
    with bones.

And now something rises, something has been released,
has been waiting, wants to breathe,
there is no stopping it, it rinses the streets of Volcano,
past the rock shop where geodes cool, and feldspar, and mica,
fills the cuff of a trouser leg, and a trench, and a silo,
out to the field where crickets clack their legs in the warm damp hay
and the stubs of sneezeweed and silverweed
call to the sky, or so I think.

A man coughs. An engine sputters and dies down. I turn
    down Emigrant,
I can hardly see Jerome. Night scours the road of detail,
of ordinary gravel, and cancels everything but form.

So that the souls of trees are unlocked. And they pour.

Time Passing, Many Afternoons

Weeds rustling,
the afternoon pulling its heat after it,
coming on like a dark hand
pulling me into the hill.

Often, I stopped to see this:
the hill drinking, and lifting its head up,
at the end, the last tree:
the dark moving the light upward.

Going home, I noticed
the comfortable shadow of the car
pacing beside me as I drove,
the cold shells of abandoned cars by the road.

As a child, I played on the lawn,
watching the afternoon gathering in a corner.
Dark under the dark elm. The latch getting dark.
The short grass, dark. My dress, soaked with it.

Working at a School for Emotionally Disturbed Children

In the morning, someone unlatched the gate;
the cows shuffled into the wrong meadow,
mooing. Everyone suspected Steve,
ten and moon-faced, for he loved to stroke their
thick, clotted fur; but it could have been Dale Allerbeck,
who set fire to the sofa, burned to a heap of charred springs.

Sometimes I would take Steve and Phil to the bayou,
where houseboats puttered up and down the water
while water hyacinths clogged propellers
so the owners would lean over their engines
and clean out the chewed bulbs, reeking of chlorophyll.
Manatees drifted by with big-lipped, moony smiles,
but Steve would be asleep, and Phil holding his fishing rod stiffly
as if he could learn this thing, *fun*.

I tried to make him laugh, but it wasn't easy:
a freakish owl in his glasses, twill coat and hat
in the Florida heat. He never went anywhere without his
    psychology books;
professorial, he was always willing to discuss his case.

And then there was Buck, who lunged for cigarette butts
and crammed them into his mouth,
swilling a whole pitcher of water,
kneeling under the coffeepot with his mouth open
so he had to be tackled and grappled in the lunchroom
by three of the strongest men,

Evelyn, weeping, her mop of hair turned to the wall,

Liz, staring at her wrists,
striped from dozens of careful cuttings,

Richard, lurching on one leg, grinning,
"Turkey-lurkey, turkey-lurkey."

At night, the sound of the rain
blurted on the tin roof: next day,
the cream-colored petals of dogwood
fell off slowly, one by one.

Mornings, I took Lester to the marsh.
Limpkins picked their way across the mud;
there were shotgun shells in the road,
rootlets, vines, Virginia creepers, big splayed palmettos,
but Lester would go on banging his head against his knee,
"ONE TWO THREE." "Lester, a snake!" "ONE TWO THREE,"
he would shout, when the lunch bell gonged,
"GO HOME! GO HOME NOW!"

Amanda, sweeping out the courtyard, full of leaves
that rasped under her broom, muttered under her breath
we were all crazy, including the staff.

There was something about the heat, thick and odorous, the grass, sopping with dew, snakes, chiggers on all the logs, my armpits and belly peppered with them, that made me restless. So I would sit hunched on a tractor, watching the ground doves in the alfalfa, the hayricks and pitchforks, listening to the cows slurp water from a tub, the rabbits restless in their cages, their feet slipping and flopping over the wires. At night moths knocked softly on the screen door, and Buck kept walking and stopping across the lawn, searching for cigarette butts, his impetigo-covered legs blotchy under the moon, his bandages flapping, night after night, like a ghost who would never get better . . .

Still, Liz stopped bringing us her wrists as if they were limp,
    exquisite flowers,
Dale Allerbeck went to college, Evelyn got well.
But Lester went on banging his head and chanting
in the same methodical way, Phil continued to wear his dark coat
on the hottest days, and speak knowledgeably of Freud,

And at night I would go for long walks,
sniffing the breeze that drifted in from Deland,
smelling of pitch pine and swamp,
and count the stars, Rigel, Algol,
but there were too many, after all,
and the light had been sent from a place
too clear, too cold, too far away.

My Grandmother's Decoupage

For Sadie Pope, 1889–1975

They stood for something, the kettle floating into a bee,
the crayfish pelted with roses,
the gull quaintly distanced from its clam;
perhaps the dream she had of painting one day,
fish, sparkling and leaping under a bridge.
She would carefully cut out a fly with her scissors,
tweaking it onto the slabs of wood,
then, with her brushes, swab the plaques with shellac,
back and forth. She took her time,
especially with the Japanese ones she loved,
geishas with spaniels on their laps and lacquered pins
shining in their heaped-up hair,
behind them a waterfall full of leaves
or a huge begonia.
She had whole drawers labeled FISH, FLOWERS, and DOGS,
LITTLE AND BIG, but she loved the fish most, I think;
because of her dream, she could see them, dace, plaice,
darters and eels, swimming under the bridge, glinting
in the muddy water.
"It's a grand life if you don't weaken," she would say,
cutting out a perch with every scale in place;
the giant locust gravely following the smaller wren,
the couple holding hands in a wreath of bees.

Walking through the Grass at Night

Past the basketball ring that sticks its face,
lonely, into the harsh light,
I walk quickly over the loud cement,
put my hand on the cold flank of a boxcar,
and as I step off into the deepest field
the grass puts on dark gloves to touch me.

A car throbs down the street and is gone,
one red light blinking.
I am alone. The odor of dark is all around me.
The cicadas are shrilling: their throats are lined with water.
It is almost November, and I am twenty;
I swim toward this loneliness with both arms open.

Long Island, 1952

I'm sorry I wasn't more sympathetic, Ellen Biedlingmaier,
when the bolts slammed outside your window
and you screamed: lightning didn't scare me,
or the rain sluicing afterwards; I liked the bravado and wet smell.
Not that I wasn't ever spooked.
I thought of you later that summer, one night
when the cinched-up canvas umbrella looked scrawny under the moon
and the glass table shone and trembled on the terrace,
rocking back and forth on its iron claws,
and the big china lettuce
that was a bowl if you took the top leaf off
wobbled and clinked in the wind;
the flagstones were icy under my feet,
my nightgown blowing,
and beyond the sharp black hedge,
bristling as it never did in the daytime,
was the sea
pouring itself over and over,
green-gold lights of the masts of boats
shining dully and oddly on its flank,
and the voices of the buoys
were the voices of the flies
I'd killed that summer with my swatter,
were the horses that threw themselves
nightly against my window,
thumping with all their leaves.

Snow, New York

In the park, between the brackets of oaks, are the other families, the tiny figures of other children, their mittens hang down like two dark spots. From here I can see sleds, and vents that hiss up steam, and delivery boys wheeling on their bikes with the big handlebars; and there is the place, when I walk home from school, that the madwoman shouts at me, hunkered over her paper bags, filling up with snow, as I hold on tightly to my project, The Flags of All Nations, my favorite, Brazil, with its blue belt and pellets of stars; and then on to dancing school, the cloakroom with its cold steel hangers and velvet coats dusted with snow . . .

Then I am walking up and down the dining room, memorizing the Wars of the Roses, and the woman across the way is in her kitchen, through the snow I can see her hands move, she is touching a fish. I declaim to the painted screens, to the Chrysler Building and its swarm of lights that revolve and prick out the names of cars, to the speckled peafowl on the walls, touching each other over and over . . .

But my mother never touches us. It is 1956. Radiators are spurting, Buicks are buried up to their hoods, snow on my glove, snow stinging my tongue, and the absence, now, of traffic, the quiet. Snow lobbing against the glass as the heat hisses up in the silence and the woman across the way is slowly being blotted out, and so are the spinning pipes on the roof and the valves and the tubs of wash sitting in the doorways, shirts clotted to the line, frozen solid and heaped with snow, and I am drawn again and again to the window while pigeons croon unhappily

from the eaves. And perhaps it is snow that falls softly and quietly be-
tween my mother and father as they sit in the living room and he whacks
open the paper with the flat of his hand and reads, as my mother mur-
murs from time to time in her sorrowful tight voice that goes on falling
and falling, burying everything with it.

Memory of Hands on a Balcony

Evening washes over the balcony
as we sit in our bathrobes, waiting.
The branches get paler.
The breath of a bird falls away,
night floods us, we lift up our faces to be kissed.
I touch my mother's hand, fretful, searching;
my father's, big as a tree, and as dark.

II

Letters to Anna, 1846–54

A Pioneer Woman's Journey

A fictional account of a pioneer woman, a native Bostonian, who moves to a homestead in Nebraska with her husband, Joel. After joining a wagon train, they cross Wyoming, Utah, and Nevada, and arrive in California in the fall of 1848.

She finally settles in Volcano, a gold-mining town, and becomes a schoolteacher.

Letter to Her Sister: Nebraska, 1846

Dear Anna,

Tonight there is a long slow cloud
moving outside the doorway like a dazed sheep,
and I miss you, miss watching the evenings with you,
falling so gently and variously.
It is all so much harder than we thought, Anna:
when we built this sod house
I never imagined the nights I would lie awake,
touching the hard dry wall,
or the locusts pelting the field—horrible.
The goat is sick. When I go in the barn
it follows me with its patient eyes
and lies in the corner and heaves:
Joel is away so much; I don't know what to do.
Do you remember that old woman, Florence,
who used to sell eggs and snarl at us, with a face
as big as a pudding?
Oh, Anna, I am beginning to understand:
just lately, when I pass the schoolyard,
the children playing make me angry,
and I want to call after them, like a crazy,
"Fools, you don't know what's coming!"
I don't mean to worry you:
there are good times.
At night the stars stitch the hills together
with such clarity I am astonished;

I like picking the cabbages,
and in the morning, when the sun falls on the floor,
the cat licks my hand;
it wants salt, I suppose, but I take it as tenderness.
Do you remember our first house in Boston,
with the piano that loomed in the corner?
I used to wake up early
and pad on those thick carpets
to watch morning enter the dark windows.
There are no windows here.
Flour is dear, and the nights are getting cold, and full of frost.
Thank you for the tablecloth.

Letter to Her Sister: Wyoming, 1848

Dear Anna,

When I woke up this morning, feeling rather poorly,
I found, in my drinking cup, a frog,
which seemed to look at me, with its dark,
unblinking eyes, with sympathy:
strange, how comforting it was.
I didn't know where to put him in all that grit, for water:
I put him in the shade; I hope he lived.
It's foolish, I suppose, but this is foolish, too:
at night I rescue the moths that flop around our lantern in the wagon,
gather them in my shawl and watch them
flutter toward the cold hills.
The ones I do not save
litter the boards like soft leaves.

On the hill in front of me this morning, are rocks, and yellow weeds,
and a few dozen grey-green shrubs,
scorched and blackened,
with woolly leaves like tongues,
and branches so twisted
they look as if they want to swim.
Never have I seen such bending and leaning;
not like the big thick elms in Boston:
do you remember the smell of those maples at home,
drenched, knocking against the house
in the rain? I do.
Sometimes I look back and think how I was at 17:

it's like reading a book about someone else:
that person who used to get up at 6 to study her grammar
to please Mr. Willard,
handkerchiefs stuffed in her pocket,
and her blouse full of ink.
How could I have worried so much about grammar.
Do you know what I mean?
My friend at the fort, Mrs. Harris, was ill with smallpox
when I went to see her—so tiny under the comforter—
her cheeks sunk, her arms pitted,
and a look in her eyes like a bitten dog.
And Eben, her youngest, looked up at me
with such a hard bright glance
so ignorant of smallpox, I turned away.
My dear, I don't mean to go on like this.
It's only, I saw a young girl at the fort,
dressed in calico, awkwardly holding the twine on her packages,
thinking the world was looking.
I thought to tell her: no one is looking.

You remember I have hurt my hip.
At night I dream of water:
wet stockings, wet hair.
I think I have fallen into the pond
at home, and come out, whole again.
I roll in the grass, and sigh with it,

careless of bruises: I fall and spring up again
like weeds under our wheels
as we pass. Nothing can crush them.
Does Daniel still go to the church?
Even I, who never believed what the Pastor said,
can find in this blue sky some kind of Lord.
I will tell you something:
when I tie up the mules to a tree,
I pray to the stars, which heal,
feeling no bigger than a shrub.

Still, my hip is much the same.
"Poultices," the doctor said,
so I have put on poultices.
It is hard for me to hoard myself,
to sit so it aches instead of hurts,
to watch how I stand; or slowly pace the mules.
Oh, Anna, I have never believed in bitterness,
and when I hear that dark wind rush at my heels,
I walk away: but it is hard.
Joel says I think too much:
it's bad to quarrel in a land as dry as this.

Letter to Her Sister: Crossing the Great Basin, Nevada, 1848

Anna,

This morning the clouds are being slowly pulled apart
by the wind, but I can't look any more:
there is something about their torn white mouths
and something still and hard about the rocks,
caverns and slag, the weight of them,
lying on my heart, that makes me lonely.
Sometimes, when the greasewood flares unsteadily in front of us,
I think it is some stranger moving;
then I remember. We are alone.
We are on rations:
Mrs. Larsen's baby is the worst: it has the colic,
it cries and cries for water,
and sucks on a rag she wets.
She shades its head and sings to it;
her throat is parched. She shouldn't sing.

Except for the sagebrush, the hills are bald.
Lizards scrabble over the sand . . .
I would sleep all day if I could.
Joel drinks less than any of us. He rides out in the dark
every morning with only hardtack for breakfast
and scouts for water. He blames himself. I wish I could comfort him.
I have to tell you: we had to throw out Mama's trunk;
we had to, it was too heavy.
For miles I thought I could hear the hasp and lock

click in the wind behind us.
It was my hope chest, too:
all those sheets you sewed for me,
the curtain with its sash
blowing in the wind . . .
Well. That is the least of our troubles.
At times the heat is overwhelming in the wagon,
and pots, tools, and boxes clatter;
it is only at night I feel at home:
when the crickets shrill and the fire sputters under our pot,
I look out at the darkness which washes up to our wagon,
and I think, this is the only home there is.
Then I forget my thirst, put out the fire,
pick the burrs from my frock, and go to sleep.
But I'm lonely, Anna, and when my hip is bad,
it blots out even the stars;
the morning's drink seems very far away.
Anna, I think of you.

Letter to Her Sister: By the Carson River, Nevada, 1848

Dear Anna,

When we got to Ragtown, we all clapped and laughed
to see that river moving in and out of those dusty hills.
The horses drank and drank, we had to stop them:
their hooves and legs looked like dark wet socks below their bellies;
I pulled on Noah's bit till it clanked against his teeth,
water slopping out of his black gums, and he still drank.
And as for us, we washed:
ears, hair, shoes sopping,
and all that caked dirt gone.
I have worn down six pairs of shoes this far,
I leave them behind me on the rocks as messages of my tiredness;
I like to think of birds making nests in their frail warmth.
At noon, when a horsefly lands on my hand,
buzzes, and cleans its wings, and a leaf
coils in the glare, it seems like it would never rain: but it does,
it rained last night. Half asleep in the wagon,
I thought I heard a moth *flop flop*
then several moths: then many.
When I woke up, I touched a pine;
the soaked bark made me shiver.
It seems so long ago that we played dolls under the piano.
I hope my letter did not make you sad.
Things get worse, and better.
It is cooler: almost September.
The clouds move slowly, like huge cold blossoms.

Letter to Her Sister: Volcano, California, 1854

Dear Anna,

I'm sitting on the porch, in Mama's gloves.
On the hill, near my house, are two trees.
One is a full tree: one is bare.
I watch that one bare tree.
Sometimes it holds the air so gently,
but I can tell: each branch aches for its leaf.

Some days, when my hip hurts, I get confused.
Part of me listens to the pain, blaring away in the dark,
and the other part is off watching.
This morning I walked out,
the fields smoked with frost,
a swallow vaulted over a barn,
the white fence seemed to go on and on,
and I thought, how good the world is, Anna.
I stepped into the shadow and stroked the cold cheek of a horse;
and the smell of vetch, and toadflax, butter-and-eggs, live-forever . . .
Now that Joel is gone, and Mama, and Papa,
I wonder, are they somewhere, singing?
I can't imagine Joel singing.
Sometimes I go to his room to look at his things:
his jacket hangs so oddly on the door,
and his shoes, Anna,
like boats, patiently waiting to sail.
I'm too old not to know we were not well matched:
at first I thought it was just me, just foolishness,

and then I saw . . . Once, in a blizzard in Nebraska,
our black calf stood and bawled in the snow.
I watched its darkness fade to white, and could do nothing.
That was the way it was. Joel's silence was the snow between us.
But he was a good man, he had such strong ideas;
when they proved false, he looked as puzzled as a child.
He looked that way the day he died,
drowned in the Mokelumne.
He knew where there was gold: he went too deep.
Now only the clouds that float so rarely by my window
are like his talk.

Anna, I thank you for your offer, and Daniel, too,
but I would suffocate in that society
I used to love.
I never was very good at being proper,
and now I'm hopeless.
How could I sit with those ladies in Boston
at a lecture or a tea?
On summer nights I wake up and think I hear
the wagons creak; then I remember: I'm in a real bed.
Strange, how I can't forget the fires sunk in the black hills,
the smell of charred dung, the sound of the horses,
guns lashed to their saddles, noisily slaking their thirst at the Platte;
how the axles groaned, harnesses, packs, jostled;
my tin cup chattered all the way through Utah.

This crossing changed me.
I look old now, Anna.
My face is cracked, like those plates I brought all the way
    from Boston.
After all the grief we've seen, it's foolish, but I mind;
I want my old face back,
the one that's mine,
that I carried so carefully through the mountains.

No, I can't go back. Besides, I'm needed here.
There's not many here that read.

I must go now. It's getting late.
Poorwills whip the evening back and forth,
and the insects, weakening in the cold,
struggle to fly.
That people *live*, Anna. I don't know.
From my window I can see an oak
with one star
like the heart, caught in its bones,
saying how easy it is, how easy
to be happy.

III

III

Waiting for You

Trying to Paint November, Waiting for You

How I'd sit, and try to paint those grey November nights,
snow, purple sky, trees running along the wall,
the yellow squares of windows
stamped in the dark.
I cut out diamonds for stars, but they were never quite sharp enough,
and really, I was waiting for you, your knock on the door, boots
    thudding in the snow,
cold air blasting as you came inside.
Then I'd clean my brushes, all stuck together, and lay out all my
    pictures of the cold,
cobalt blue, burnt umber,
an elm with a spine that clamped a star between each branch . . .
and you would say they were good or bad, or needed a little here,
    or there,
frost floating off your shoulders,
your cold hands around me under my shirt, so I would jump,
unbolt the latch, shut the two doors, radiators knocking and clanking
    behind us,
Miss Daykin's voice, high and querulous, crabbing on the phone
    through the wall,
pad down the stairs in my thin shoes, leaves crashing, snow biting
    my feet.
We could hardly look at the stars, it was so cold,
but felt them, made our way to the car, heads bent:
then you would lay your head by mine and I would stroke your fine
    white hair and breathe,
and at each breath, your hair would lift: then we would kiss,
and look out at the ice.

Christmas Morning without Presents: The Depression, Granite City, Illinois

It is 1929. The moon falls on the floor,
the pantry is empty, beans hardening in the cans.
No, you did not expect this.
The same cracked wall with its stains,
odor of your mother's cleaning fluid,
curtains with their clean hems,
blowing in and out.
You touch the bones and lumps of the chair,
the broken wireless with its dial, you pick up a spoon,
and it's cold. A clock ticks. The chipped plates
fill up with the moon.
You look back at the window,
tubes and vats of the factories
quiet for once.
The garbage truck rolls up the alley,
the bristles of the streetcleaner's brush rasp on the pavement.
Your hand closes on the doorknob, quietly.
You begin to carry the stone of your childhood:
The moon. The empty room.

The Lake, Two Years Later, without You

Succession . . . occurs when organic matter builds up at the bottom and around the edges (of a lake). In time, a forest, the climax stage, develops. . . .

—Taylor Alexander and George S. Fichter, *Ecology*

The cows are still the same, of course, banging their cowbells and heaving into the shade, leaving behind boggy hoofprints where tree frogs huddle every year. But the tree frogs are different, and so are the mallards, daughters of the daughters of the ones we saw, and the bullhead are different, and the trout, and the log we used to sit on crumbles from the weight of my boot, wood chips and dust flying, while dazed carpenter ants scuttle about, trying to plug up the holes.

I thought it was odd, you lifting my hair, counting the grey ones. Teasing, I thought, but it's true. Succession, they call it, when the lake fills up, duckweed and silverweed, cinquefoil and silt: alderflies, dobsonflies sinking like flakes, and the scales of hoary catfish trawling with their mouths, and the tiny hairs on the backs of the legs of backswimmers and water boatmen; gum from the willows, and the narrow leaves of Sagittaria, all pointing in one direction; the lifeless shells of dragonflies and damselflies, their leg hooks still holding desperately to a reed, but finally skinnying down into the water, and floating, and drowning.

Snail shells, snares and lures, the quarter-ounce lead weight sinkers and the half-ounce; caddisflies, and the cases of caddisflies; wings, and the shiny wing cases of beetles: dust, dirt, and pollen, all that drift and fill, reeds advancing from the side so that it will eventually become a marsh, and then a meadow, and then fill with trees, and that will be the end, there is nothing after trees.

The Case for Solace

Port Townsend, Washington

A holdfast is the root of a seaweed, which often anchors it to the
sea bottom by wrapping around a stone.

I go down to the beach, with its lengths of kelp,
one with a holdfast clutching a pebble.
It doesn't matter how small it is, the harbormaster says,
it does the job.
I don't miss you so much. I'm surprised.
Maybe it's because the sky is always changing,
cumulus to stratus, stratus to altostratus,
altostratus to rain.
At the Grebe Dive Shop, the black rubber suits
and flippers smell pungent, and the divers advise
against the tide. Shark stories, and cases of beer.
At night I sleep calm,
hearing the cutters and scows,
the moan of the buoys and the put-put
of the huge, rusted *Ginza Star* as it switches engines
and enters the strait.
Maybe it's the rain, it doesn't matter how small it is,
or the swallows, flying around my ankles in the cut grass,
picking up bugs my feet release.
On the cliffs, ailanthus and clover fall straight down to the water.
It's summer. I forget what else should matter.

IV

Alive with the Others

The Dead

The dead come, looking for their shoes.
It's all right if we can't find them:
it was only the dark, inside, they wanted.
It's all right. They can be the shadow of a boulder,
or the oak leaves falling, one by one.
There have been so many of them, and so few of us.
The ones we loved take our hands in the morning
and watch us:
Eyes in the river.
One day we will be like them,
and rise, like waves, out of the hot fields.

Alive with the Others

Mist rises from the lake, one layer unpeeling at a time,
and the lake speaks for the deep recesses of slag and rhyolite

fish barge and prowl in these waters, the old jaw-boned fish,
mullets, lungfish, with their fins borrowed from hawsers and files

turtles, with their snouts, sprawl on a log
snakes count each other in the water

and the brilliant thrushes
spread into a leafy cluster

Trees, each with its neighbor,
hear them each to the other in the night

beech, maple, elm, hickory,
each with a different slap of leaf

the way my sister and I used to sing to each other
I under the coverlet
she behind the dark bolster

beyond question there is enough light

the rock is moving so slowly inside
but it is moving

Kinds of Darkness

Every night the maple rocks against my window:
it is a dark horse, quiet, and full of blood.

Over and over the sea pours its sieves;
its mouth, calling me, is dark and alone.

In a grove a long way off
there is one house with a light:
shape of a lamp, and a big chair.

My father's coffin lowers into the black hole,
and the flag falls after him,
the last skin of darkness he could hold.

Sky

Do the dead float there, though we cannot see them
do they bathe their arms in the blue, near the shore
for it is not true the sky has no shore

though sometimes it is only gauze, unrolling
length by blue length

as when we were children
we stood in the store, in the musty corner
touching the sofas
the stiff bolts of cloth
stroking the painted birds
the dahlias

in the immense boredom of childhood
the adults were talking of wallpaper and chintz

the blue came through a little square window
and looked at us

and on the long ride home
the seats of the Buick scratching our thighs

it was the blue driving alongside

or was it my father, walking across the lawn
in his tall dark coat, smiling
as I held out my French book

Texas Nursing Home: A Visit from Her Son and Seven Daughters

Momma lay in the bed, looking small and frail. By her side was an open Bible, and the brittle paper kept making whispering noises in the wind, while the curtains blew in and out, and they could all hear the jets of the sprinkler spurting *phut-phut* onto the dry grass, and the *coo-roo, coo-roo* of the ground doves as they scratched in the pokeweed and gravel.

Evelyn's husband, Wendell, had decided not to come into Momma's room, as the room was small, and he wasn't family. So he sat outside on a small chair, and through the visit they could all hear the clink of his cuff links as he mopped his brow, and his voice as he chatted with the nurses, "Well, now, that's a heavy load."

The trouble was, no one knew how to begin to say what they wanted to say to Momma.

And so they all stood around, the seven sisters with their hats and suits and dresses, clutching their purses and handkerchiefs, their stockings whizzing against each other as they shifted from foot to foot, when Tony, looming over the bed in his huge blue suit, sat down and pressed her hand, thin and dry as a leaf, between his two large ones: "How are you, Momma."

And she, as if recalled from some distant place: " 'Mm all right."

Coo-roo, coo-roo, the ground doves kept up their noise outside the window, picking up pieces of tansy, goosefoot, and crab grass, a plane droned across the sky, and a radio blared and quieted as a door opened and closed.

"Why, Tony," she said. She lifted her hand so slowly they all watched it rise, touched his hair, let it float back down to the sheet.

"Why, Tony, your har—your har's grey."

"I'm fifty, Momma, fifty," he said, catching her hand, while behind him the sisters swayed and shifted in the room, as if a breeze had passed through a fleet of sailboats and left them gently bobbing on the water.

Someone she didn't remember was holding out a flower. A tall blonde girl. Well, they were all tall, the Darrows.
"It's Ellen, Momma—you know, Tony's chile'. She brought you a flower."
It was a wilted morning-glory, the head flopping down, undignified. She rallied.
"Put it out thar . . ."
"What, Momma?"
"Put it out thar in the field and let it grow."

V

Advice from an Angel

Advice from an Angel

1

Today I saw one of those Digger Pines you love so much,
uprooted, its needles in shambles,
tan, flaking,
and the wheel of its roots
still holding clods of dirt:
twenty kilometers of roots
tangled in that vast shelf,
a thousand kilometers
of root hairs and nodules
delicate as the teeth of radishes,
bulbs, tubers,
and embedded in bits of loam and hornblende,
unseeing, staring,
the tiny blind eyes of pebbles.

2

I know you're afraid sometimes.
But that's all right. It's those voices from childhood—
quarrels, drinking—the sound of the ice
knocking in her glass as she stumbled down the hall
towards your door. It's understandable. And the glacier
does look frightening up there on its cirque,
with its hooks of ice. But down below
are the fields and pastures full of vegetables;
cauliflower squats in the caked earth,
its blue furred leaves smelling of rubber,

and there are tubs of melons,
cranshaws, summer squash,
potatoes dug from the loosened soil,
dropped in burlap, smelling of mold,
still spotted with dark crumbs . . .

3

If I have any advice, it's this:
watch the moon as it rises with all its money
and spends it carelessly on drift and cirrus,
but above all, love
                    the packed earth,
loaded with coal,
boles from the old carboniferous swamp stumps,
slivers of chalk, shells of molluscs,
boreal slopes, bitter escarpments, shale, hardpan,
alluvial gravel, bits from the early seas:
holding the powdered bones of cattle,
holding the old shoals.

4

Below the stump, where the bluebird sits and preens
its chest, and crooks its wing, and flicks, and preens,
below the stones, below the rubble of the sink,
under the glacial erratics,
where springtails leap and scatter in the snow,
ten feet down, where cold toads
bivouac between clumps, away from the wind shear,
and earthworms steer towards each other through the dirt
and lie wrapped in balls for shelter,

below the centipedes, millipedes, where the ants
and the silverfish wander,
under the slump of crust where the heat thuds,
nickel and magma, and the pulse of the core ticks as a watch ticks,
there is a calm hand,
the palm facing down.

   5

I know it's in your nature to want air,
ozone. To float: to be free. But stick with what you know:
you'd be surprised at the effect of sheer blundering
and doggedness. To evaporate is nothing:
to sprint, to travel. It's weight
that divides the known and unknown worlds. It's your boots
that impress us, your squads of boulders,
and your heavy wadded soil. And in your oceans
it's those blue blots
we notice, the shadows of clouds
that float like tanks
and make the sea look deep,
while all around, the turquoise
shallows dazzle, and the sea-lettuce sparkles,
and the kelp . . . Do you remember
on the tablets in the graveyards in Rome,
the matrons hold out their hands,
and their dead sons kneel under them.
Those hands: it was their weight you noticed,
and when you looked down,
loosestrife and mullein
                    bungled up between the graves,

someone pedalling by chinked a bicycle bell,
and, under your shoes, the grass sprang up,
already busy, repairing itself.
Didn't you notice how heavy you were?
It's the same weight
that pulls down
                    birds from the air, leaves, boulders,
anything that falls.
And there is so much falling.
From up here we can see them, the dark lines
attached to every living thing, and then to the soil.
They look like strings, or pulleys.
But it's all right. It connects you with the earth, and all its grit.
Would you believe me if I told you it was all
all right? Look: a calm wave of heat
blows through the breccia and sandstone,
a calm wave of light. Clouds release their arms.
Across the ridge, dusted with little feathery Diggers,
rock doves clatter and disappear, and clatter back again.
The quality of hope is bent, and lies in the light sweet sand.

About the Author

Ellery Akers is a teacher, an artist and writer, and a naturalist. This book was written partly in the desert, partly along the Emigrant Trail in the Sierras, partly in the Gabilan Range, and partly at writers' colonies at MacDowell and Ossabaw Island. She has led field trips for the Audubon Society, San Francisco State University, Sonoma State University, and the Nature School, College of Marin, and has done research at Point Reyes Bird Observatory.

Akers lived in New Zealand as a teen-ager, where she joined a repertory company, then left for Radcliffe College, from which she received her B.A.; she earned an M.A. from San Francisco State University in 1974. She has worked as a photojournalist in Vermont, picked pears in Norway, and studied art. Parts of this book won awards from the Poetry Society of America: the John Masefield Award (1980 and 1984) and the Gordon Barber Award (1985). She received an Academy of American Poets Award (1974). Her home is in San Francisco.

About the Book

Knocking on the Earth was composed in Bulmer, a twentieth-century typeface named after William Bulmer (1757–1830), an English printer best known for his printing of a fine edition of Shakespeare. The book was composed on a Mergenthaler Linotron 202 by Brevis Press of Bethany, Connecticut. It was designed and produced by Kachergis Book Design of Pittsboro, North Carolina.

Wesleyan University Press, 1989